Goodness Me, Mr Magee!

T0359973

Written by Jill Eggleton
Illustrated by Sandra Cammell

Mr Magee put
the pigs on his truck.
"We are going
to Mrs Joe's house,"
he said. "Mrs Joe
likes big fat pigs."

Mr Magee went
down the road.
He saw a coffee shop.
"Good!" he said.
"I will get some coffee."

Pig One looked out
of the truck.
He saw trees and flowers.
He saw grass and mud.
He got off the truck
and ran away.

A mouse came
over the grass.
It went up the wheel
and onto the truck.

Mr Magee came
back from the coffee shop.
"We are going
to Mrs Joe's house,"
he said. "Mrs Joe
likes big fat pigs."

Mr Magee went
down the road.
He saw a lunch shop.
"Good!" he said.
"I will get some lunch."
And he went into the shop.

8

Pig Two looked out
of the truck.
He saw trees and flowers.
He saw grass and mud.
He got off the truck
and ran away.

A mouse came
over the grass.
It went up the wheel
and onto the truck.

Mr Magee came back
from the lunch shop.
"We are going
to Mrs Joe's house,"
he said. "Mrs Joe
likes big fat pigs."

Mr Magee came
to Mrs Joe's house.
"Mrs Joe! Mrs Joe!"
he shouted.
"I have the pigs!"

Mrs Joe looked in the truck.
She looked and looked.
She put on her glasses.
"Goodness me, Mr Magee!"
she said.

"What little pigs!"

A Map

Guide Notes

Title: Goodness Me, Mr Magee!
Stage: Early (2) – Yellow

Genre: Fiction
Approach: Guided Reading
Processes: Thinking Critically, Exploring Language, Processing Information
Written and Visual Focus: Map
Word Count: 234

THINKING CRITICALLY
(sample questions)
- What do you think this story could be about?
- Why do you think Mr Magee is taking the pigs to Mrs Joe's?
- Why do you think the pig wanted to get out of the truck?
- Look at page 6. Who do you think Mr Magee is talking to when he comes back to the truck?
- Look at page 12. Why do you think Mrs Joe had to put on her glasses?
- Look at page 14. What do you think Mr Magee will have to do now?

EXPLORING LANGUAGE

Terminology
Title, cover, illustrations, author, illustrator

Vocabulary
Interest words: coffee, wheel, flowers
High-frequency words (reinforced): put, the, Mr, on, his, we, are, going, to, he, said, house, likes, big, a, good, will, get, some, from, back, have, me
New words: road, what, want, little, saw, away, ran, shout
Positional words: onto, off, over, into, down

Print Conventions
Capital letter for sentence beginnings and names (**Mr M**agee, **Mrs J**oe), full stops, exclamation marks, quotation marks, commas